CREATE 'N' RACE
MASTERBUILDERS

This book belongs to:

.... Mrs Nault ....

Age:

....

A LEGO Media Book

 media.

First published in the USA in 2000 by LEGO Systems Inc.
555 Taylor Road, P.O. Box 1600, Enfield, CT 06083-1600

Reprinted in 2000

10 9 8 7 6 5 4 3 2

ISBN 1903 276195

Colour reproduction by Elements
Manufactured in China by Leo Paper Products Ltd.

Check out other cool toys in the LEGO Technic range!

CREATE 'N' RACE
MASTERBUILDERS

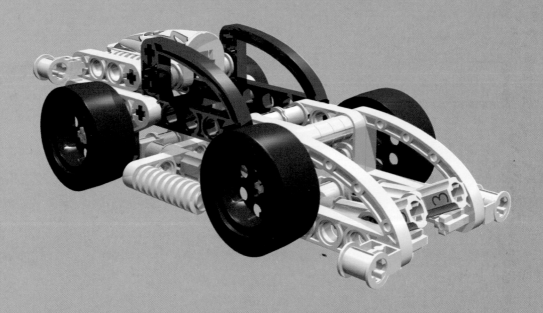

Illustrators **Alexander Tomlinson,**

Sebastian Quigley and Jason Edwards

Author **Davey Moore**

Managing Editor **Anne Marie Ryan**

Senior Designer **Stephen Scanlan**

CONTENTS

NUMBER OF MODELS   14

Smell the gasoline, hear the roar of the engines, grip the steering wheel – and GO! This is motorized mechanical mania that you can build yourself! You'll have a "wheelie" great time creating a 300 mph dragster, a rough ridin' motocross bike, a monster truck and a mean and nasty jeep.

Create 'N' Race will show you how to become a LEGO Masterbuilder. Specially developed with the help of professional LEGO Technic model-makers, this book lets young apprentices like you learn from the experts. Work your way through the cool models featured in **Create 'N' Race** and you will be a Masterbuilder in no time at all!

The models in this book range in difficulty from easy, to medium and difficult. Try warming up with the simpler models before tackling the more challenging vehicles. Special symbols on each page will show you the level of difficulty and how many bricks are used in the model.

All the LEGO Technic elements you need to make each model in this book are included in the plastic box. Before you start building a model, it is helpful to find all the bricks that you will use and place them in front of you. Store the bricks back in the plastic box when you have finished building so that they don't get lost.

There are fourteen amazing models to make in this book, but that is just the beginning. You can try designing your own cars, bikes, trucks and crazy off-road vehicles with real working steering, suspension and pumping pistons. Go anywhere, build anything – as fast and furiously as you like!

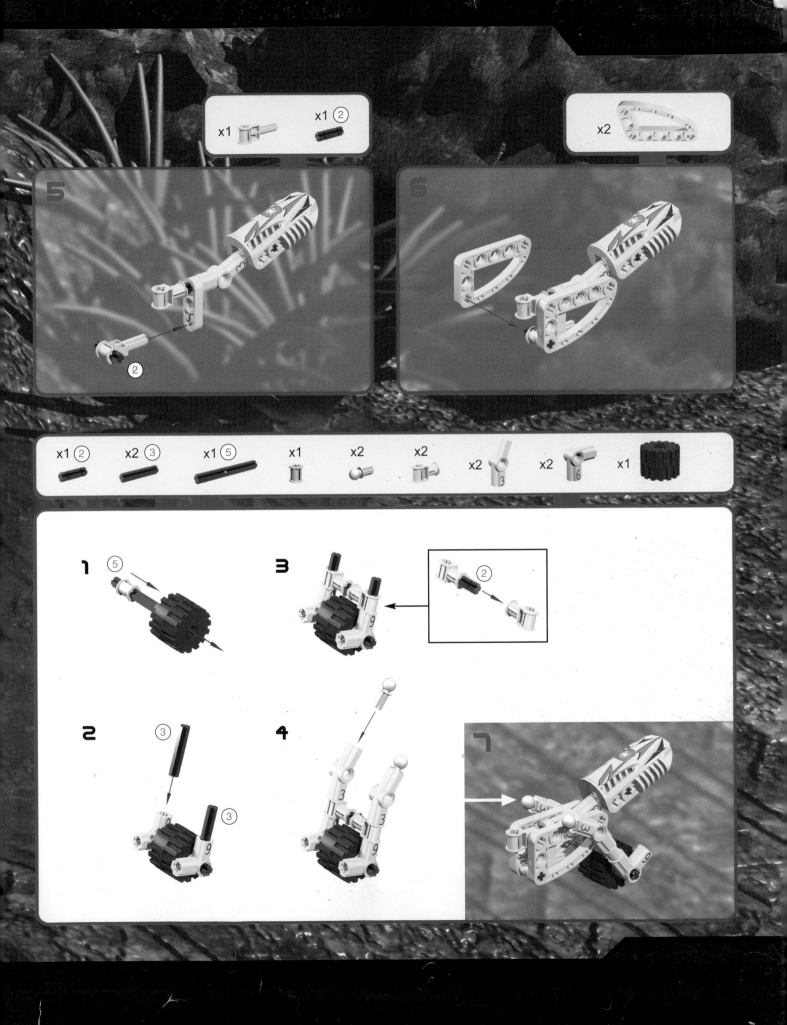

4

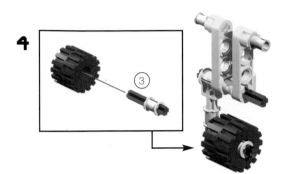

③

5

Scrambler SPECS

Engine type	Two stroke
Engine capacity	249 cc
Dry weight	222 lbs
Wheelbase	58.2 "
Ground clearance	12.8 "

9

x1

10

A trike is any vehicle with three wheels – but don't mistake this powerful machine for a child's toy! This vehicle is born to be wild. With a low-slung seat and a rear weight bias, this three-wheeled monster is tricky to tame. At rallies, speed isn't the only area of competition. Trike owners try to outdo each other with flashy paint and body work. Once you've built this trike, try customizing it with other bricks.

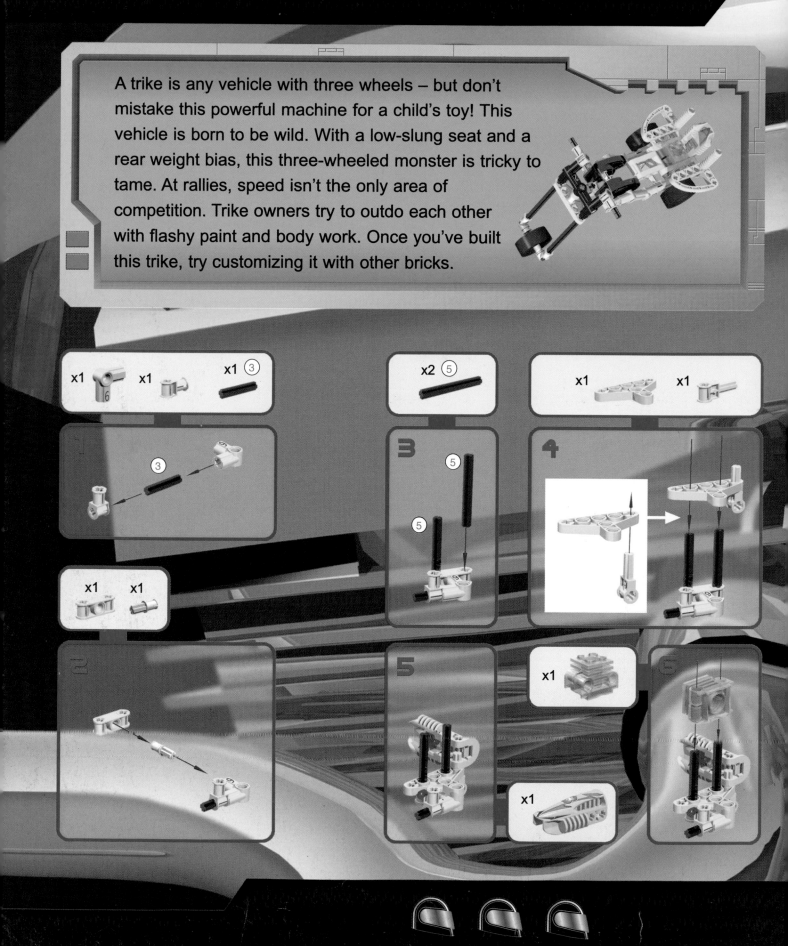

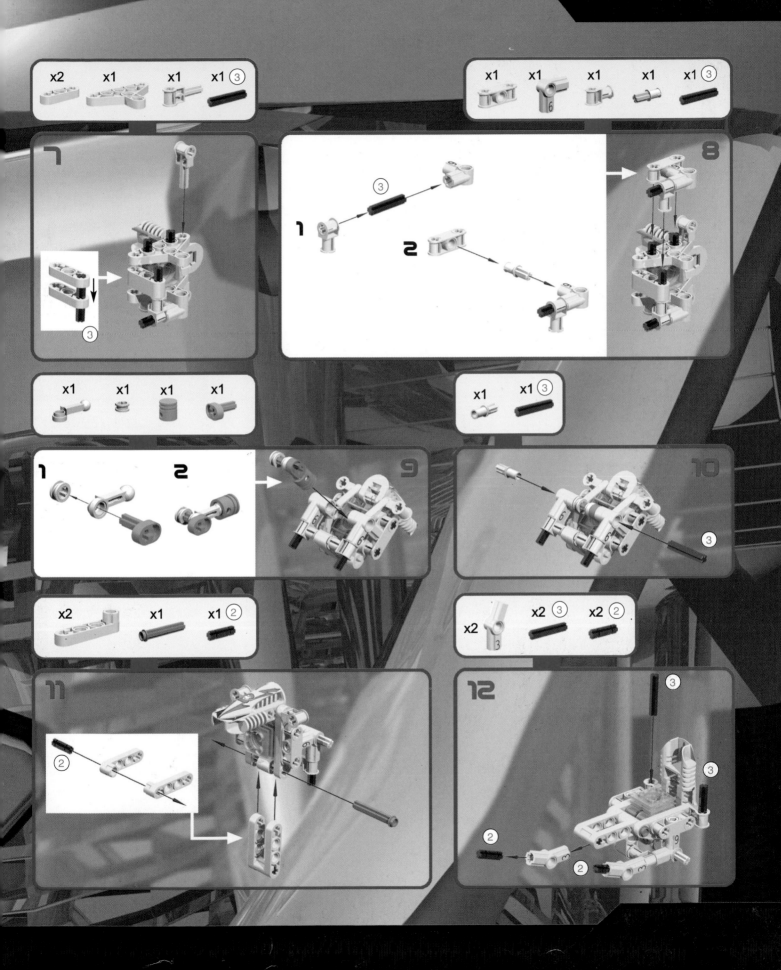

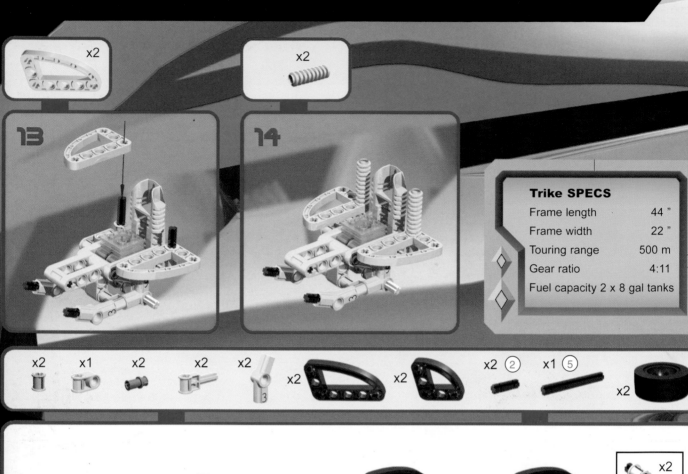

13 x2

14 x2

x2 x1 x2 x2 x2 x2 x2 x2 ② x1 ⑤ x2

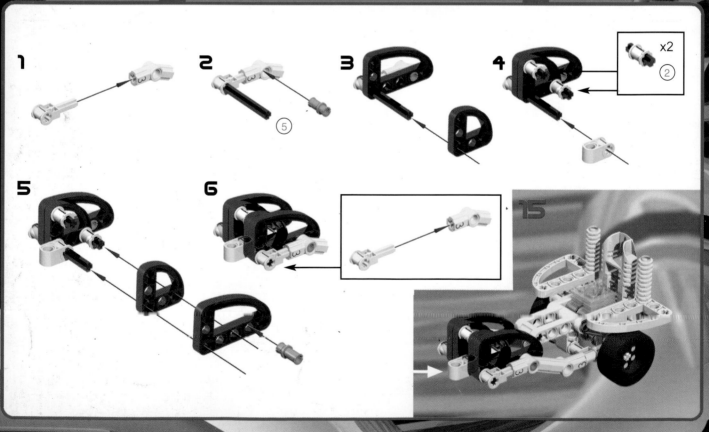

1

2 ⑤

3

4 x2 ②

5

6

15

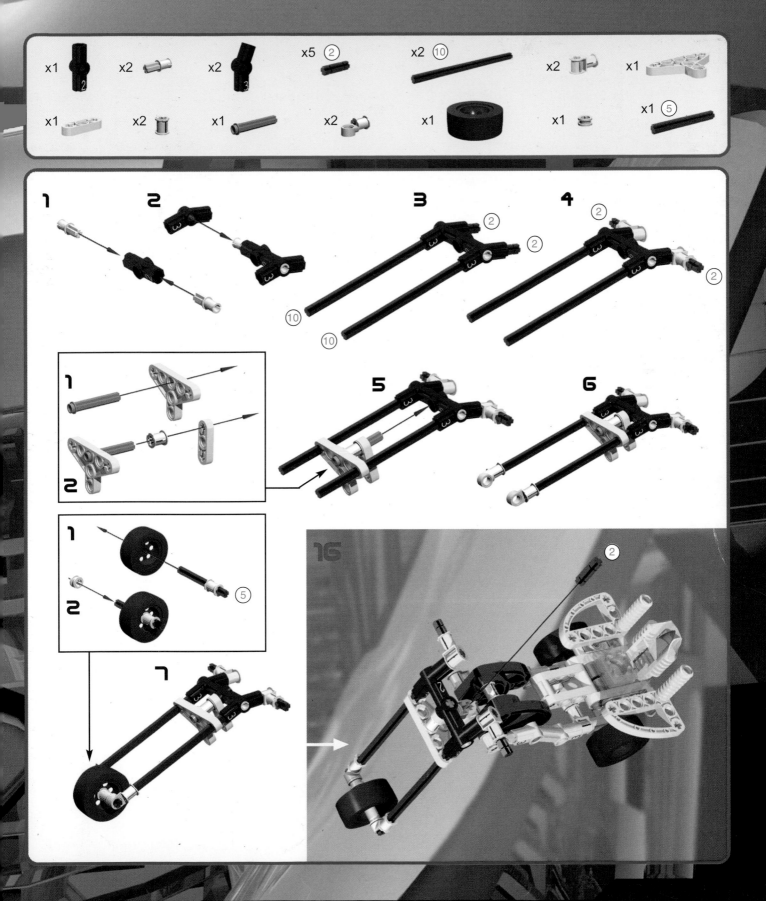

Car racing is one of the most glamorous, adrenaline-pumped sports in the world. But sleek Formula 1 cars and fierce, fast dragsters are not the only vehicles that race. Many motor sport events use souped-up versions of cars that you see in the street. Car racing is not only confined to race tracks, either. Road rallies take place at night-time on normal public roads. Customized dragsters with their large wheels and individual bodyshapes are called funny cars. Why not try making souped-up versions of these cool cars by customizing them with extra bricks?

Rally Car
Unstoppable! What this chunky rally car lacks in size it makes up in power! Head straight for the finish line!
Page 22.

Hot Rod
Leader of the pack! Come rain or shine, this jazzy little hot rod will give you a run for your money.
Page 20.

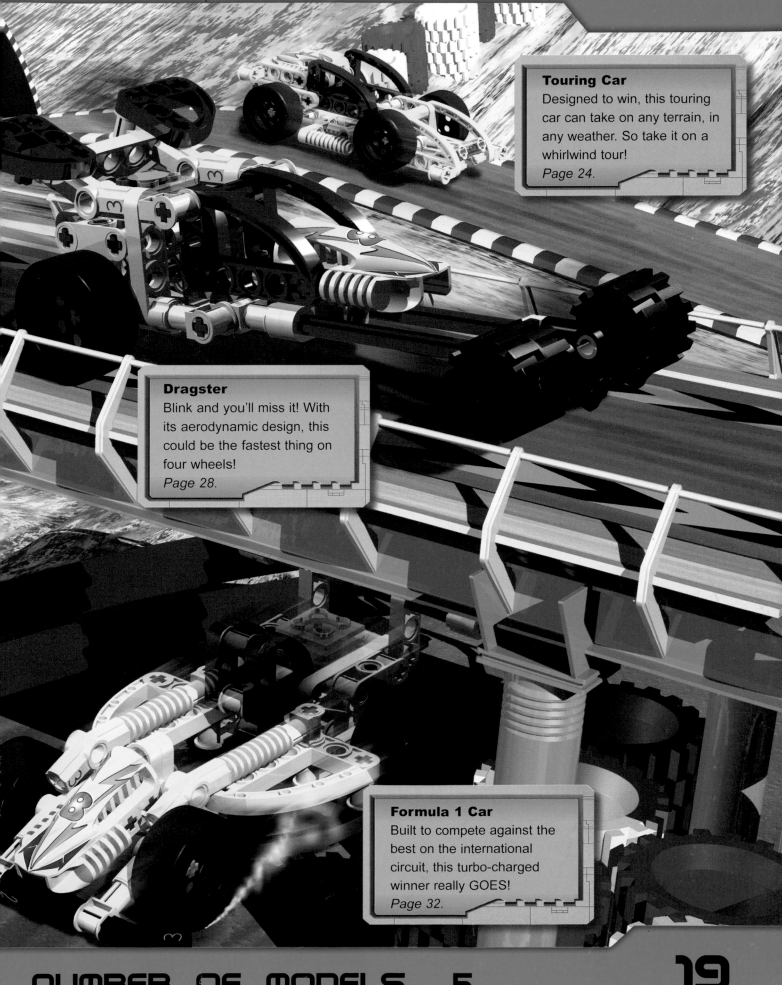

Touring Car
Designed to win, this touring car can take on any terrain, in any weather. So take it on a whirlwind tour!
Page 24.

Dragster
Blink and you'll miss it! With its aerodynamic design, this could be the fastest thing on four wheels!
Page 28.

Formula 1 Car
Built to compete against the best on the international circuit, this turbo-charged winner really GOES!
Page 32.

NUMBER OF MODELS 5

20 HOT ROD

This hot rod may be compact, but it really can motor! The small front wheels and exposed engine give this hot rod extra speed and power. Overtaking the pack, it remains in front, lap after lap. Your bricks can build both this hot rod and the rally car on the next page at the same time. Why not pit the two cars against each other in a top-speed race to the finish line? Which car will claim the winner's trophy?

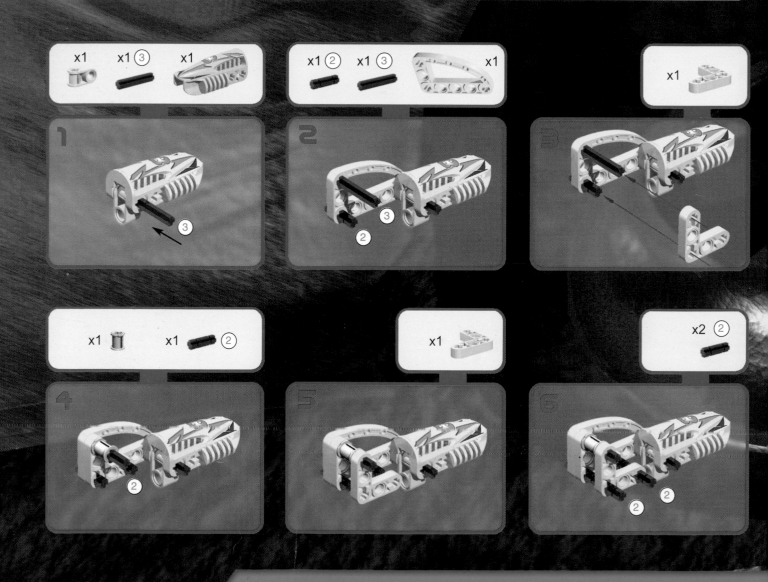

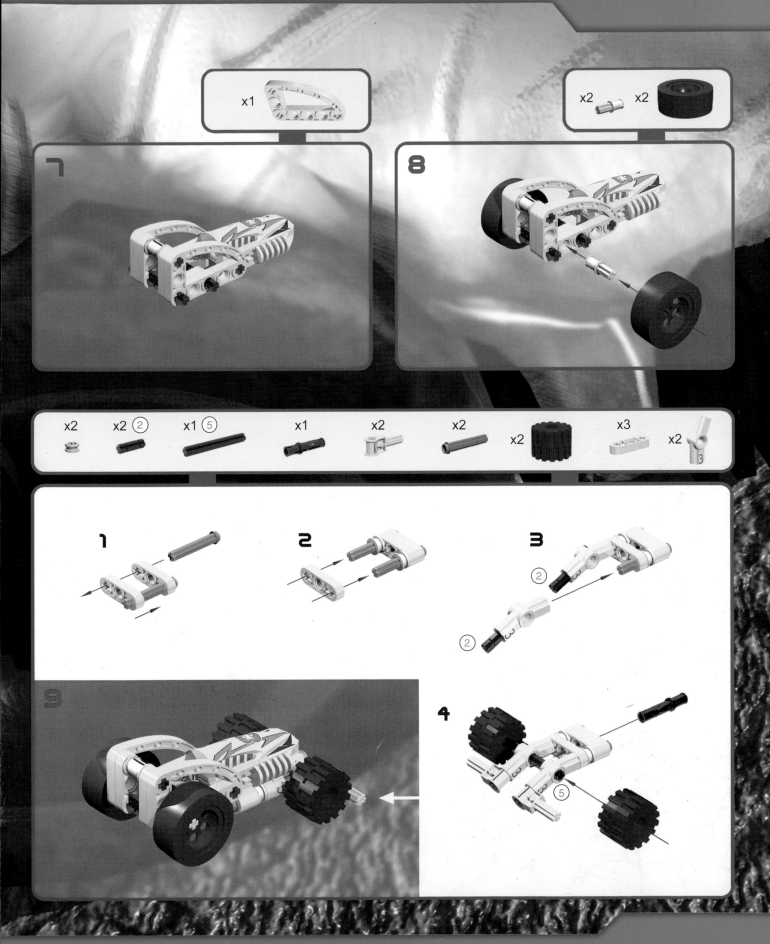

Rally cars are tested for speed and endurance. Put this beefy car to the test. Devise a rally route and see if a friend can follow your directions in a set time. Or, using the hot rod from the previous page, challenge a friend to some timed trials – sprints and hillclimbs are popular events. If you like extreme motor sport, hold a stock car race, where the aim is to crash into the other cars. Which will be the last car driving?

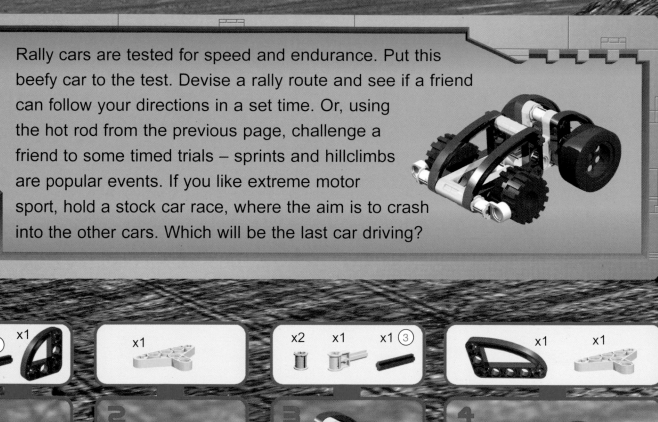

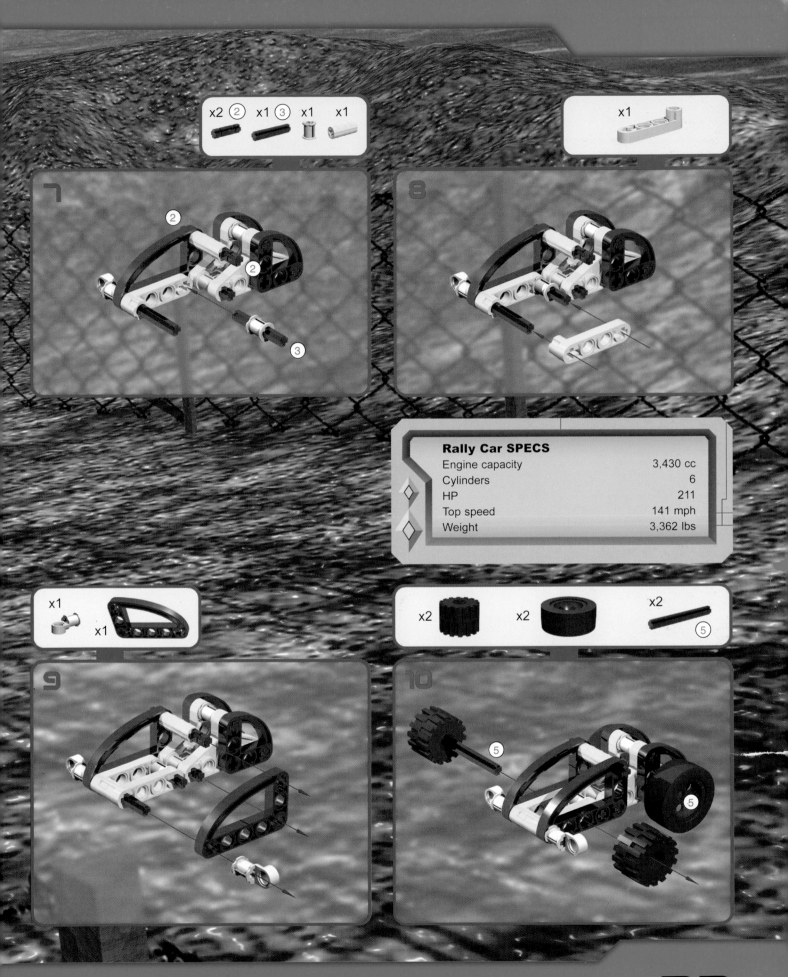

Rally Car SPECS

Engine capacity	3,430 cc
Cylinders	6
HP	211
Top speed	141 mph
Weight	3,362 lbs

24 TOURING CAR

From the outside, touring cars are not unlike vehicles you might see on the road – but on the inside they are built to win, wherever they race, from sandy deserts to snowy trails. Try mapping out your own race course on some paper. It makes no difference if it's fast, flowing and full of long straights, or tight and twisty with plenty of sharp bends. This touring car can take on any course, in any weather!

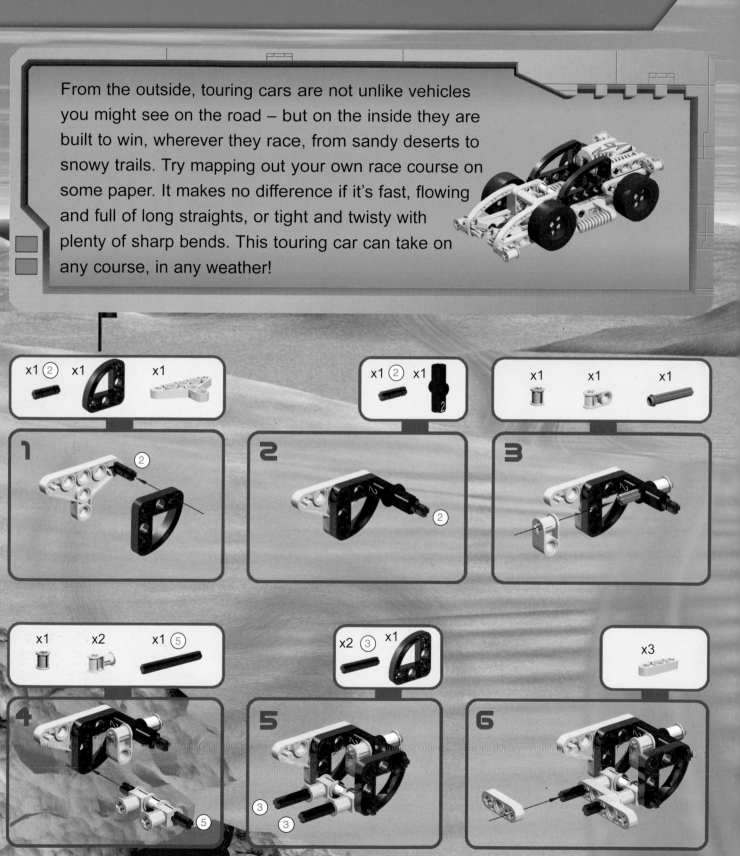

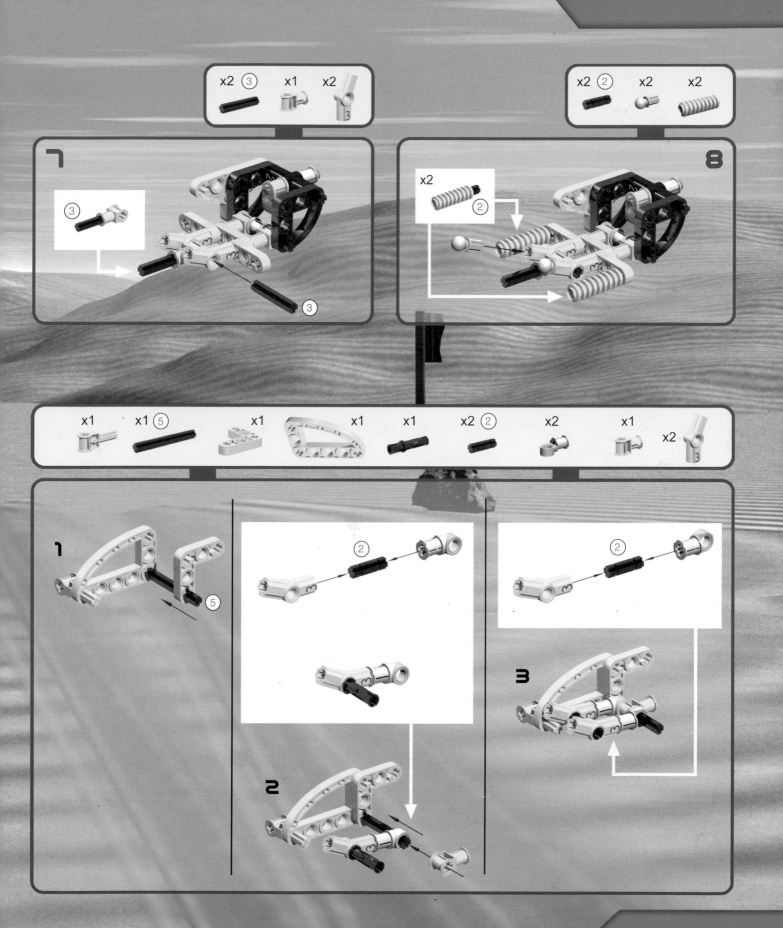

26 TOURING CAR

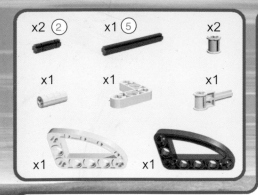

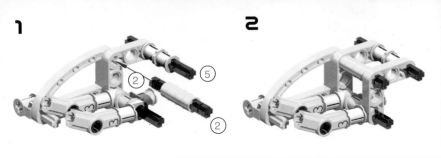

1

2

9

3

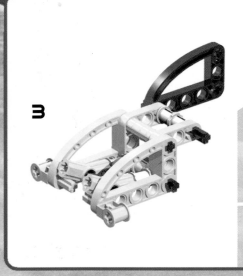

x1 ⑤

10

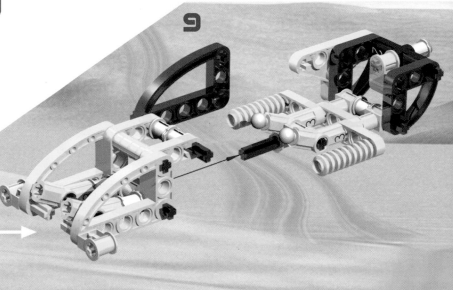

x4 ②   x2   x2   x2   x1   x1   x1

11

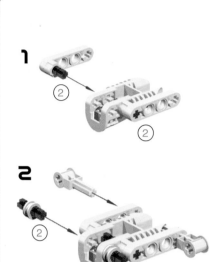

1

②

②

2

②

②

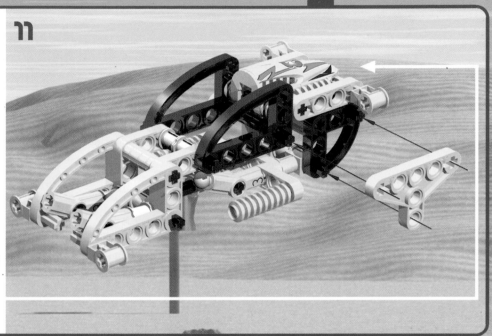

x4   x4

12

Touring Car SPECS

Torque	200
Tire size	18 x 8.5 "
Weight	2,161 lbs
Top speed	160 mph
Transmission	6 speed

28 DRAGSTER

Dragster racers speed down the straight, quarter-mile strip as fast as they can in the shortest possible time. Burning rubber, this hot rod accelerates from a standing start to over 300 mph in six seconds. Drag is the resistance a car meets as it cuts through the air. This dragster has small front wheels to reduce drag. Dragsters slow down by releasing a parachute. Attach a handkerchief to your dragster's tail to make a parachute!

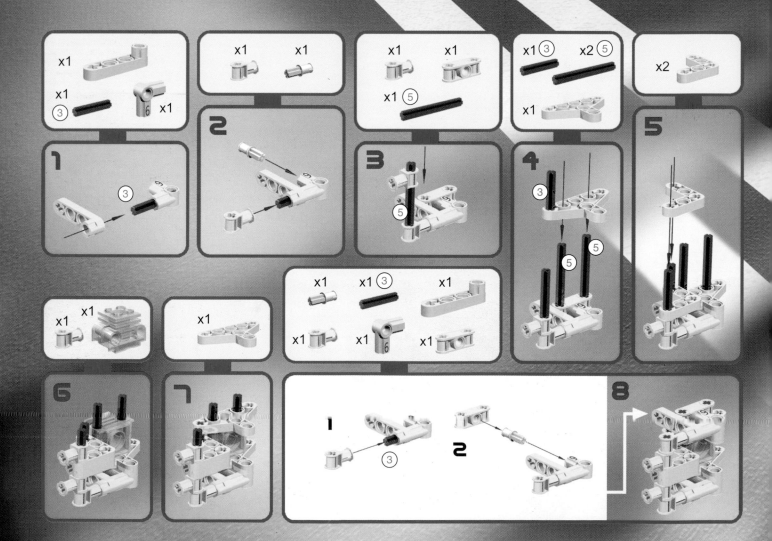

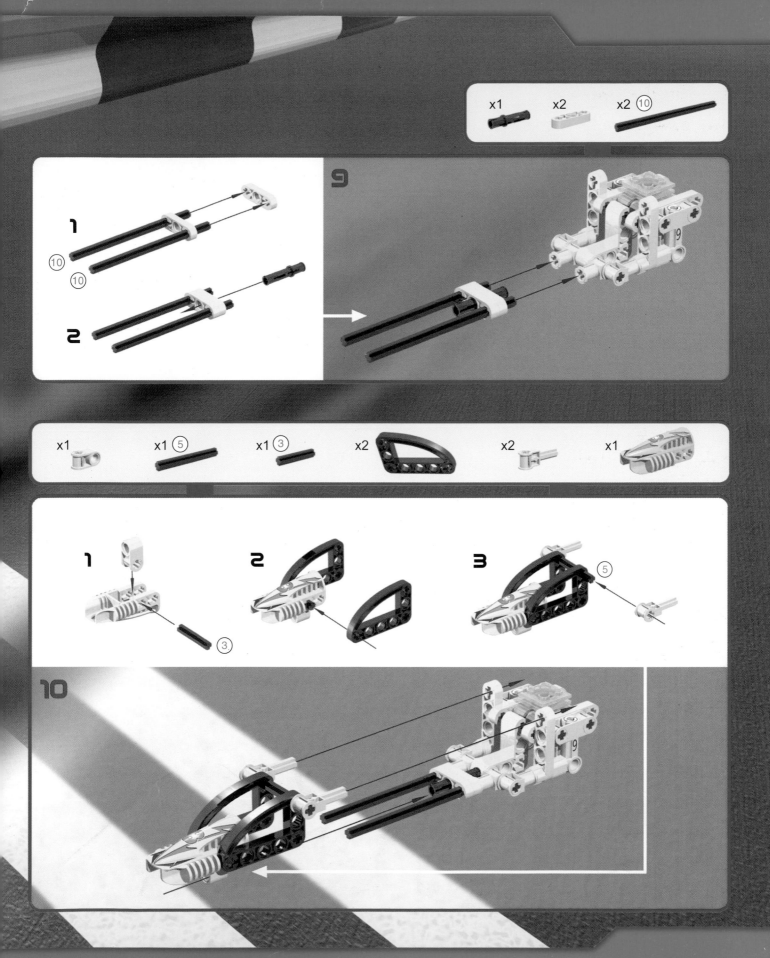

x1　x2　x2 ⑩

9

1
⑩
⑩

2

x1　x1 ⑤　x1 ③　x2　x2　x1

1　2　3

③
③
⑤

10

9

30 DRAGSTER

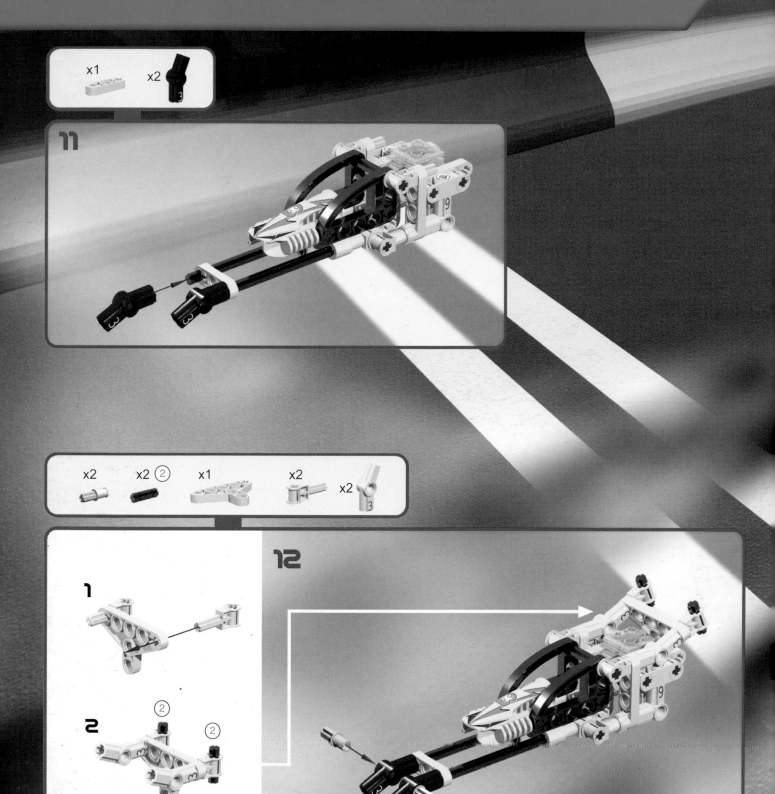

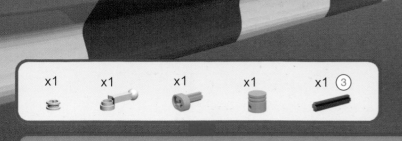

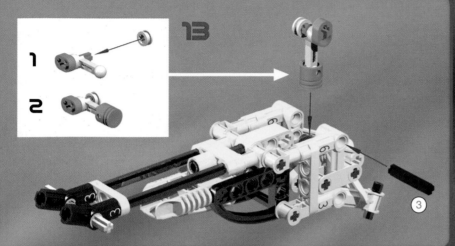

Dragster SPECS

HP	6,000
Fuel capacity	13 gal
Weight	2,125 lbs
Thrust	6,500 lbs
RPM @ speed	8,350 @
	326 mph

32 FORMULA 1 CAR

In Formula 1 racing, drivers and their teams race around a circuit at top speed, competing for the title of world champion. Formula 1 cars are designed to be as aerodynamic as possible, but there are strict rules about safety. Grooved tires reduce daredevil spills and crashes, and the chassis provides roll over protection. But this is still a very dangerous sport. How far will you push the limits to win?

x1 ②   x1   x1   x3 ②   x2 ③   x2   x2   x2   x2

1

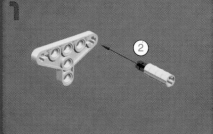

②

1 ③   **2**   **3** ③

4   **5** ② x2   **6**

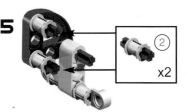

2

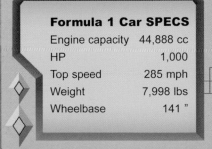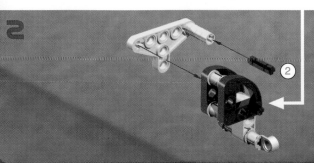

②

Formula 1 Car SPECS

Engine capacity	44,888 cc
HP	1,000
Top speed	285 mph
Weight	7,998 lbs
Wheelbase	141 "

LEVEL

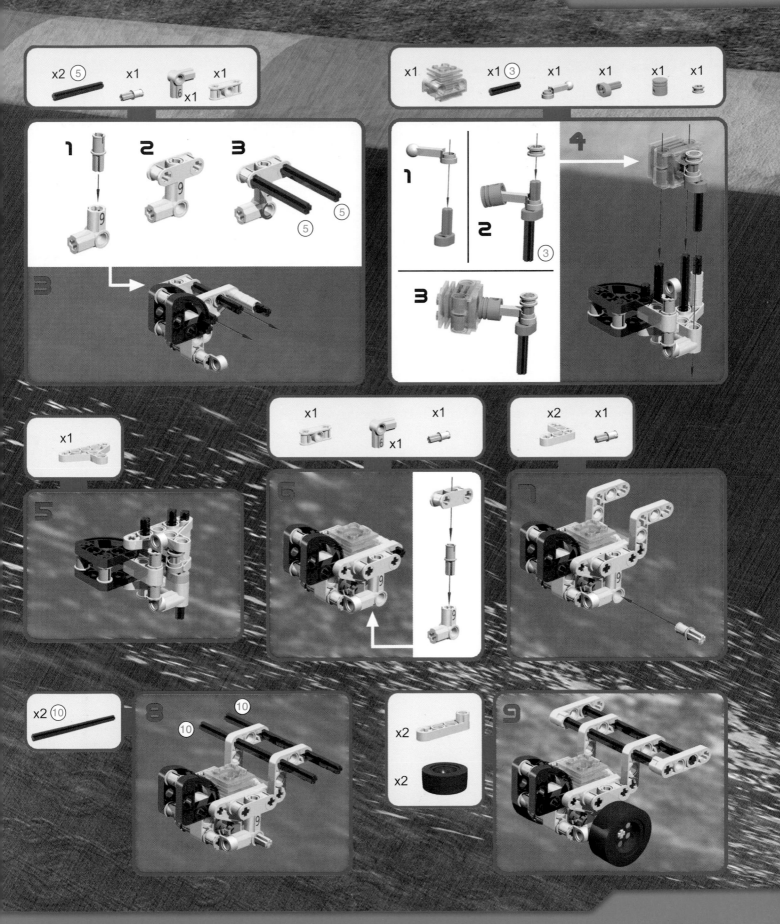

34 FORMULA 1 CAR

LEVEL

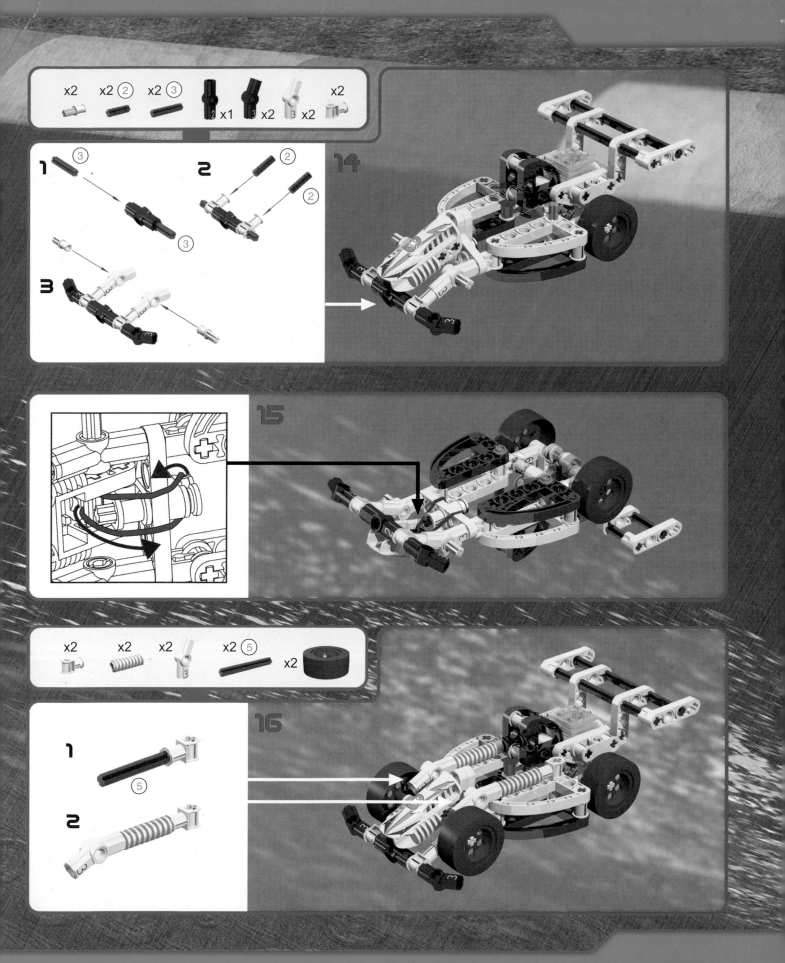

DC TRUCKS

Truck racing has something that no other form of motor sport has – a speed limit! The finest trucks could probably reach speeds of 140 mph. But the 100 mph speed limit makes this sport about control rather than just slamming the pedal to the metal and going flat out. Truck racing is one of the safest motor sports. Trucks are raced on unbanked circuits and, when accidents occur, it's likely that more damage will be done to the track than to the driver! Of course, sometimes a racing truck is written off, and that's when the tow truck and dump truck come into their own!

Racing Truck
Unbeatable! This high-speed truck's too elegant to put on the road. It's built for competition, so get it racing!
Page 44.

Tow Truck
Bang! Crunch! When there's been a crash, this strong, solid tow truck can haul away the debris.
Page 48.

Monster Truck
This mega monster truck will scare off all the competition! As it leaps through the air, the crowd goes wild.
Page 38.

Dump Truck
Practical and powerful, this dump truck can build a race track, deliver new tires or perform amazing tricks!
Page 40.

Monster truck drivers love to show off their mighty, mean machines at fairs and rallies. Monster trucks are all about extremes – extreme power, extreme noise and extreme action! This monster truck is a customized pick-up with super chunky tires. The oversized wheels and real working suspension make it ideal for showy tricks such as driving over lines of scrapped cars – ker-runch!
To what extremes will you take your monster truck?

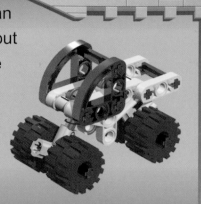

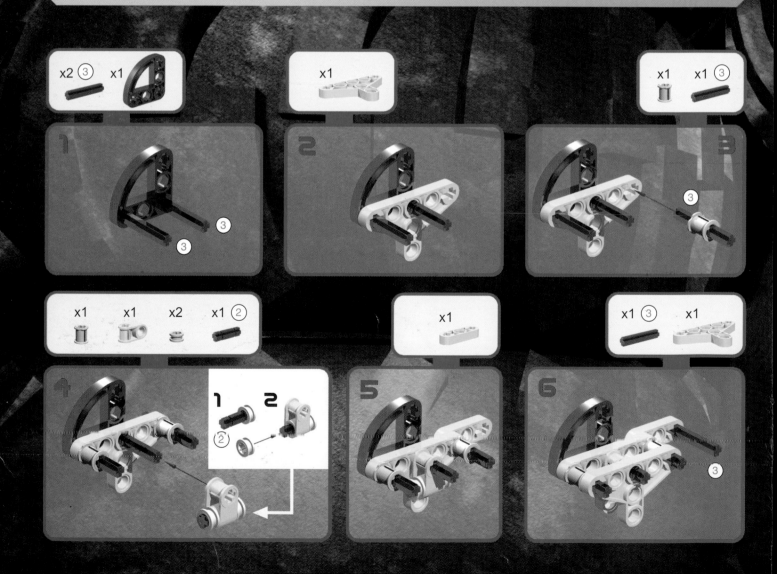

x1 ② x1 x1

x1 ③ x1 ② x1 x1

7

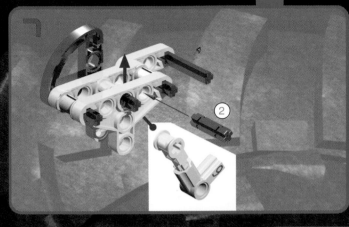

②

8

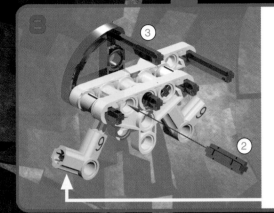

③

②

x1 x1

x1 ○

9

10

x2 ⑤

x4

11

⑤

⑤

Monster Truck SPECS

Weight	6,860 lbs
Maximum tow load	7,940 lbs
Ground clearance	32 "
Wheelbase	130 "
Grade capability	80%

40 DUMP TRUCK

Before vehicles can be raced, a track must be built. What better way to haul sand, soil and cement than with a dump truck? Try transporting some bricks and planks to build ramps and jumps! This dump truck really works, so tilt back the rear to drop off a load. In the USA, star truck drivers perform amazing tricks with these metal giants in truckster rodeos. Try making your dump truck do a wheelie!

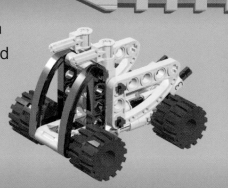

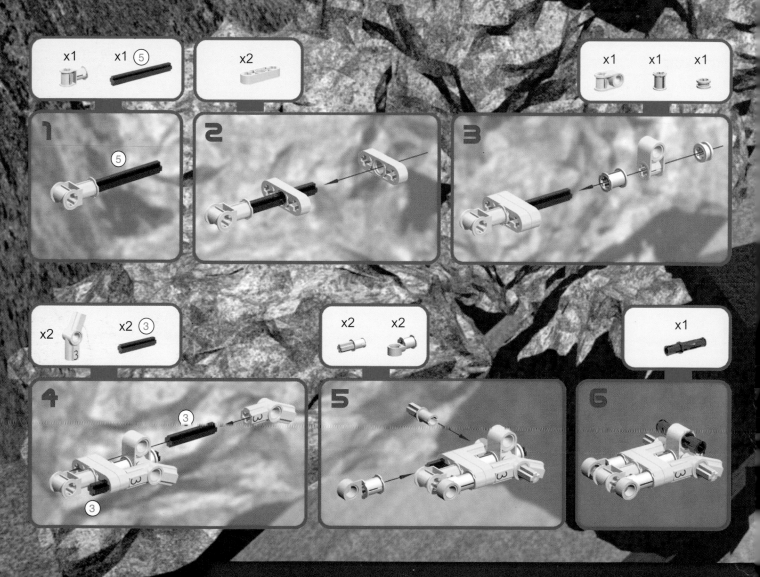

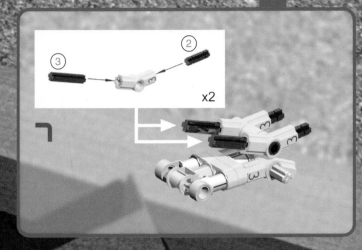

7

 x2 x2 ⑤ x2 x1 x2 x1

8

1

2

⑤

⑤

3

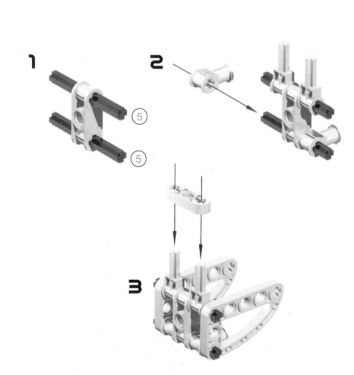

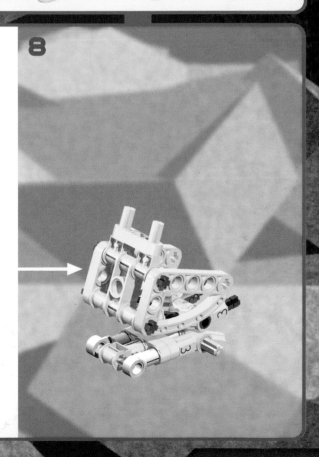

42 DUMP TRUCK

x2   x1 ⑤   x2 ③   x1   x2 ②   x2   x1   x1

1   2   3

③ ③ ③   ⑤

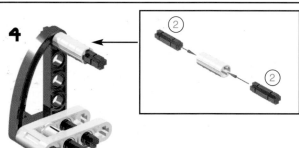

4   ② ②   5

6

x4 x2

10

This racing truck might look like the big vehicles you see chugging down the highway. On a race track though, this truck can do up to 135 mph. That makes for some cool competitions, with roaring engines and burning rubber! You can create tire-scorch effects by pooling a little black paint on paper and driving your truck through the paint. When the paint is dry, you will have some tire-screechin', rubber-smokin' burn-outs!

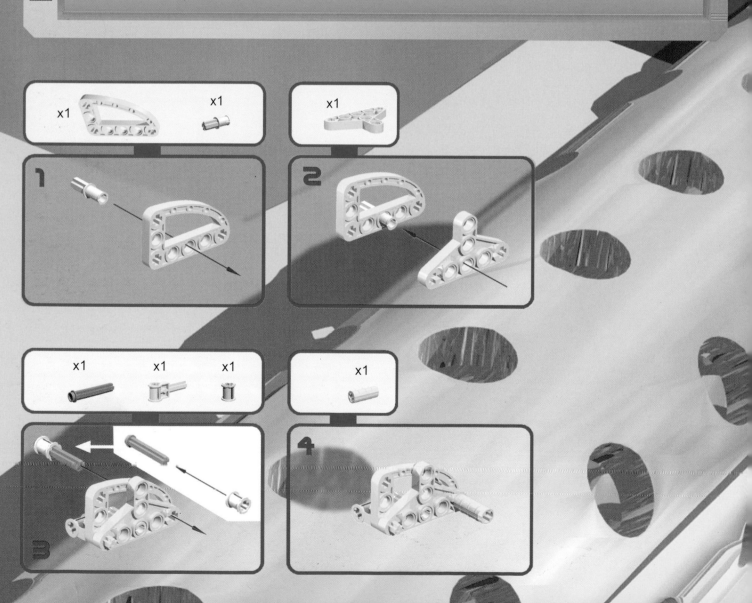

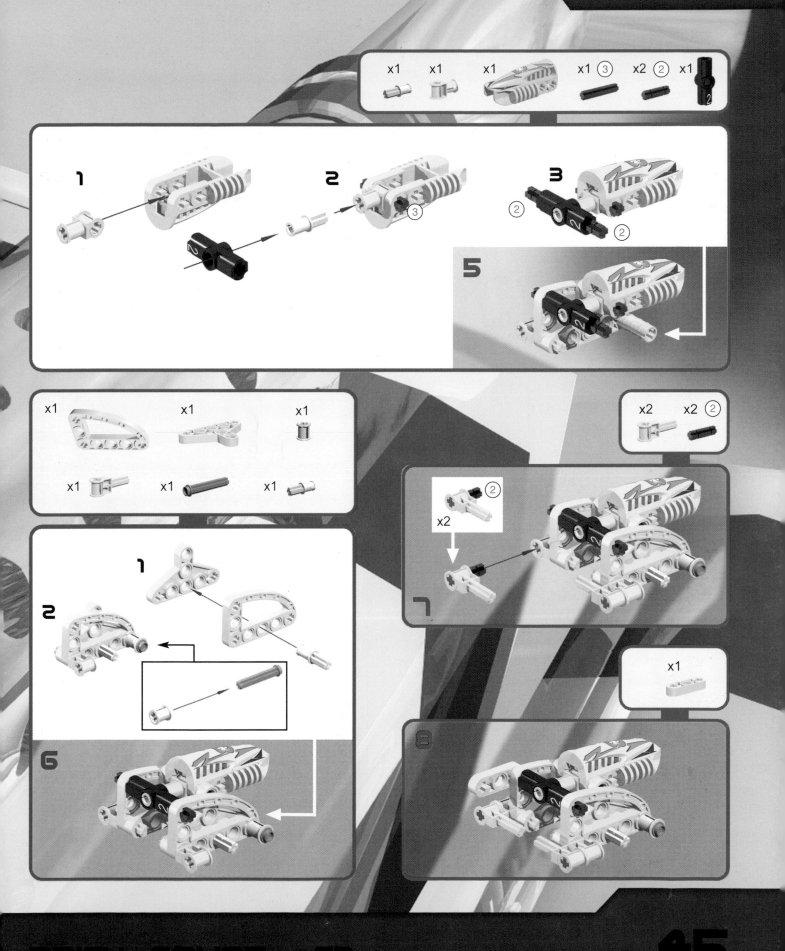

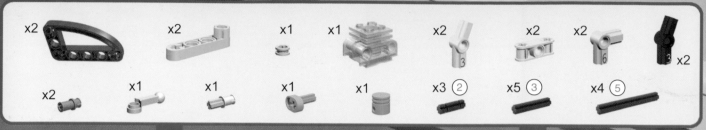

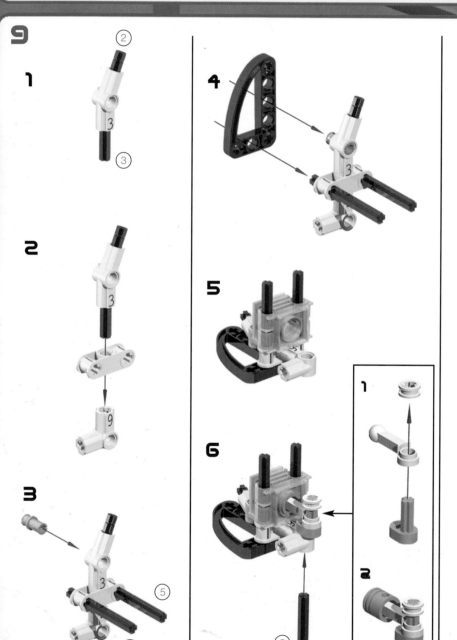

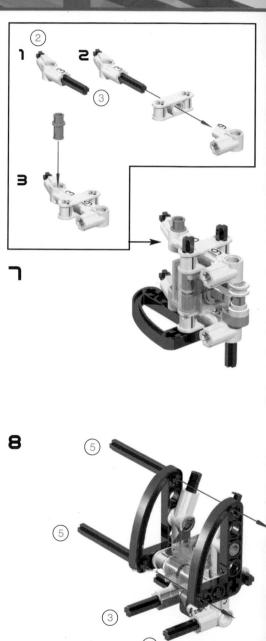

9

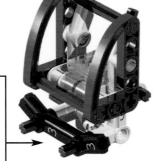

x1

10

x4

10

11

48 TOW TRUCK

If a car crashes at speed, it can do some real damage! When a race car is completely wrecked, it's time to call for a tow truck! This tow truck has extended-mobility tires to help it reach the scene of a crash, no matter where it is. It can even run 50 miles after getting a flat! You can use this articulated tow truck to haul away the remains of a stock car race. Or invent a new sport – tow truck racing!

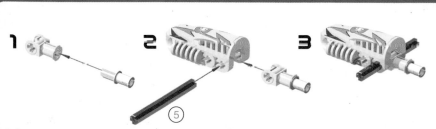

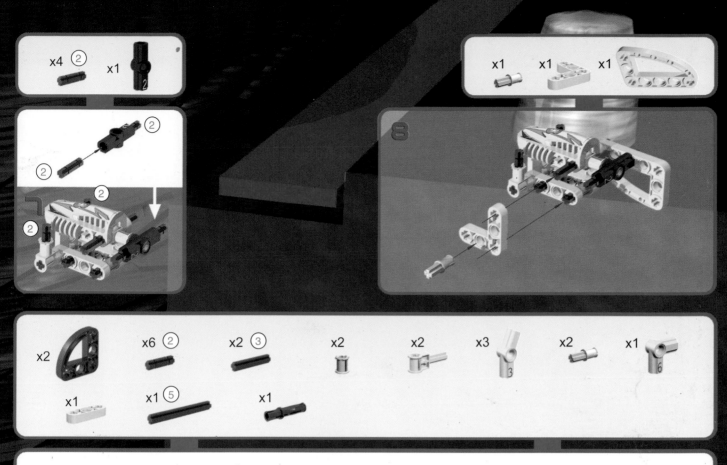

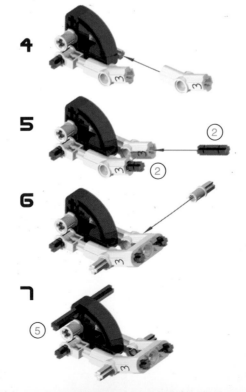

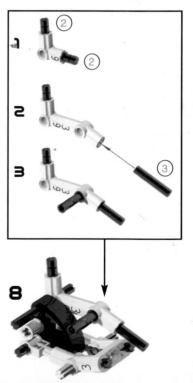

50 TOW TRUCK

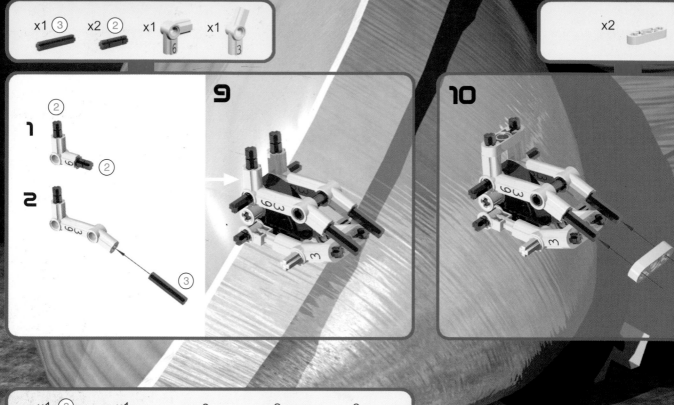

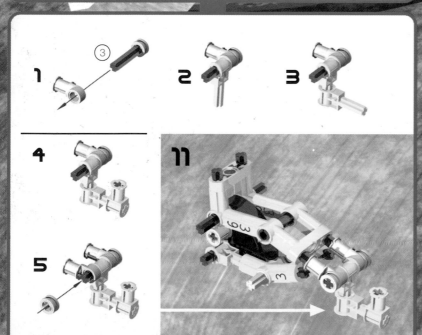

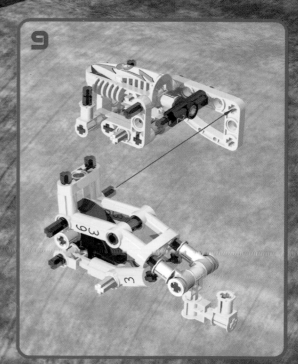

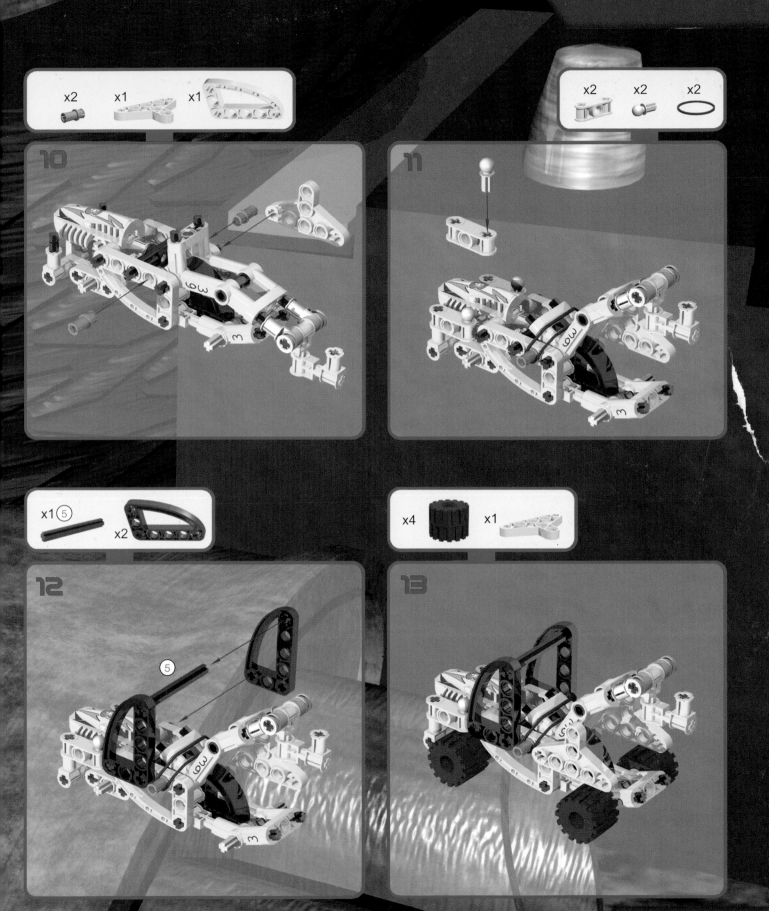

Imagine conducting the power of your engine to four wheels instead of two – that's the excitement of 4 x 4 racers! With 4 x 4 vehicles, you get twice the power and double the action! So take your trials of speed and control off the asphalt surface and get out of the city. Are you ready to confront nature's own race course? Whether faced with rugged rocks on a mountainside or the sliding sand of a desert dune, 4 x 4 racers can take on any surface! Get ready to go off-road and race a jeep across a desert or haul an immense load with a mighty tractor and pull!

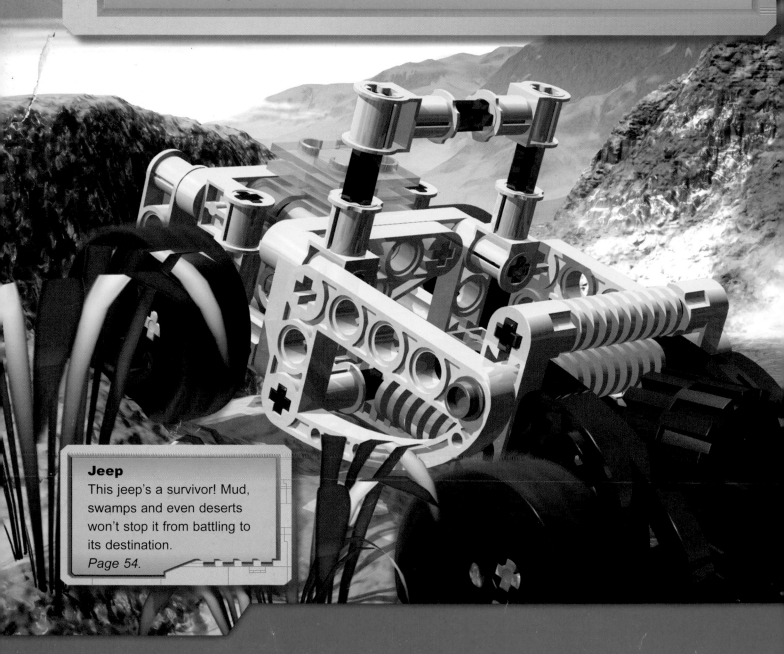

Jeep
This jeep's a survivor! Mud, swamps and even deserts won't stop it from battling to its destination.
Page 54.

Tractor
Heave ho! Traditionally a farm vehicle, this tractor can pull in prizes at motor shows! It's slow, but it has awesome power!
Page 58.

Trailer
Just along for the ride! Build a trailer for your tough tractor to pull along in tractor pull competitions.
Page 60.

JEEP

The jeep has earned its reputation as an unsurpassable rescue vehicle in the world's disaster areas. Jeeps can go anywhere, through floods and hurricanes, battling against the elements. They are also great fun to race! Build your very own racing jeep complete with a pumping piston engine. Then construct a ramp and see how many LEGO Technic bricks your robust jeep can jump – good thing it has a roll cage to take the shocks!

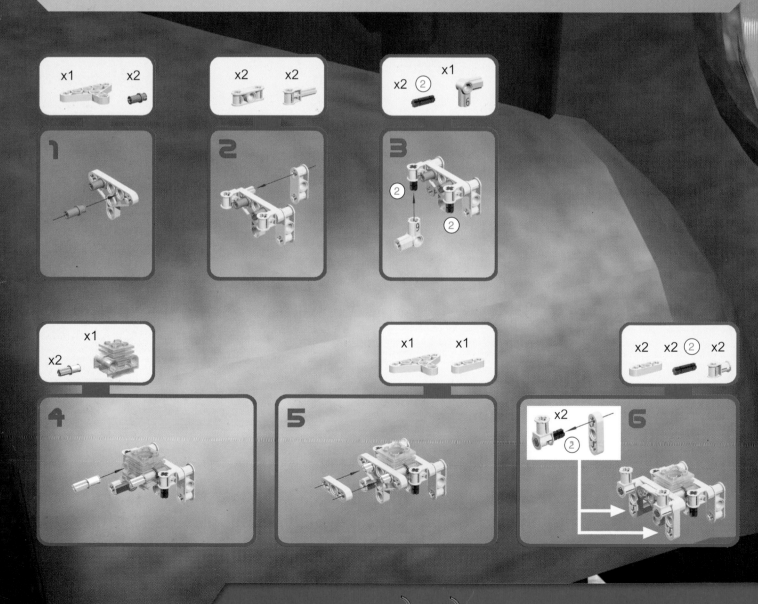

56 JEEP

x1 ⑤   x2   x1

x1   x1

x1   x1 ②   x1   x1

14
⑤
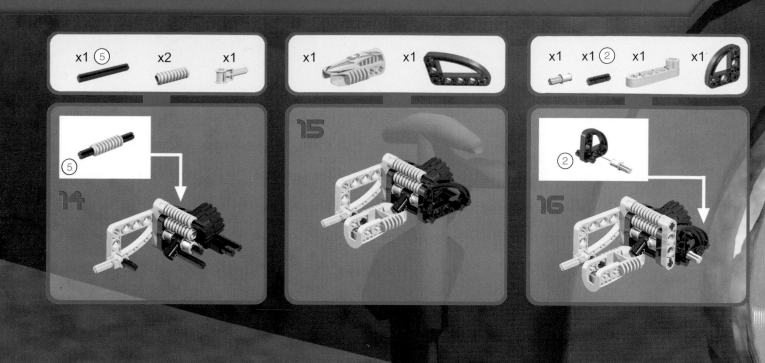

15

16
②

x1 ③   x1   x1   x1

17
③

18
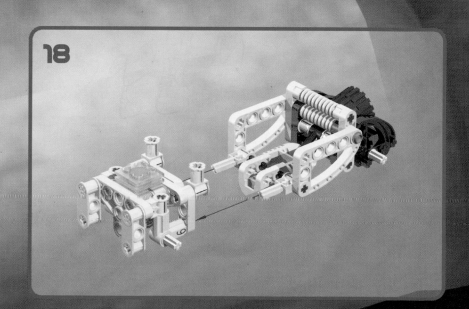

Jeep SPECS	
Wheelbase	103 "
Length	147 "
Width	71 "
Height	58 "
Transmission	Electronic four-speed automatic

x3 ③   x2   x4

1   ③   2   ③   ③

19

58 TRACTOR

Slow, but mighty powerful, this tractor's far more than a
farmer's friend. This vehicle is full of pulling power!
The large tires at the back are designed for maximum
traction. While this added friction slows the tractor down,
it also helps pull the tractor out of sticky situations!
Create deep ruts in mud or sand and make your
tractor eat up the pits and troughs! You can even use the
rest of your bricks to build the trailer on the next page!

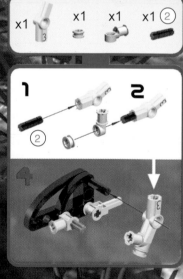

Tractor SPECS

Wheelbase	70 "
Length	115 "
Width	64 "
Turning radius	96 "
Weight	2,450 lbs

It's time to test out your tractor's pulling power! You can build this sturdy trailer after you make the tractor on the previous page to create your own tractor and pull. The trailer can hook to the back of the tractor, so you can move heavy loads across even the most treacherous terrain. See how many bricks the trailer can carry over a measured distance. Start off with a few and build up to a massive pile!

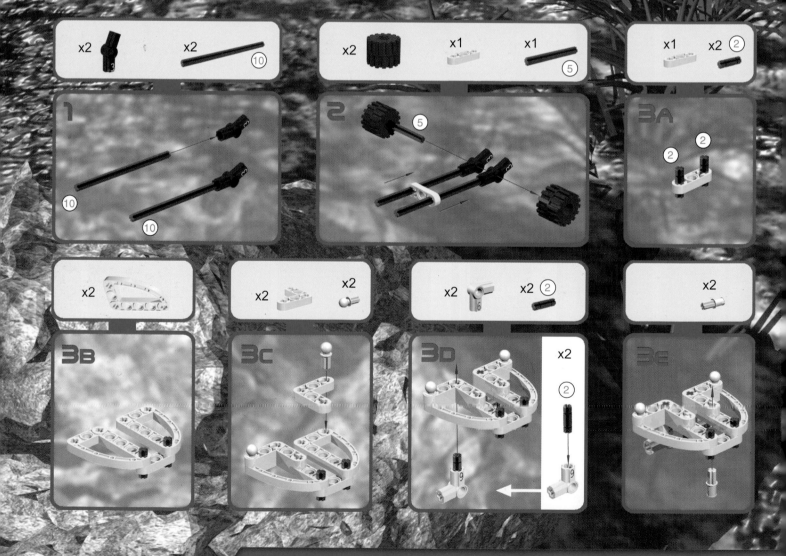

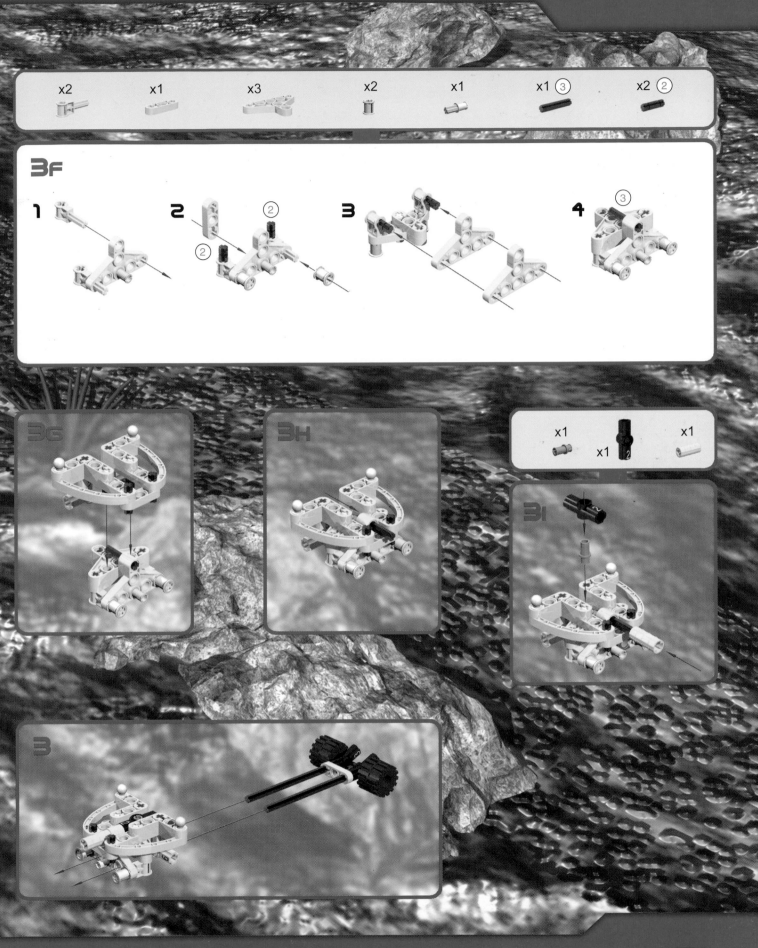

62 TRAILER

x1   x1 (5)

x1 (3)   x1

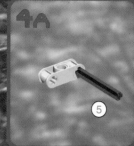

4A

4B

(5)

x1 (5)   x1   x1 (3)

x1   x2 (3)

4C

(5)

4D

(3)   (3)

x2   x1 (3)

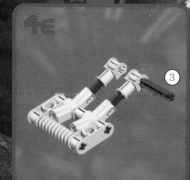

4E

(3)

Trailer SPECS	
Maximum tow load	7,750 lbs
Ground clearance	16 "
Tyre size	19 x 9 "
Length	123 "

LEVEL